There Is Only Now

A Simple Guide to Spiritual Awakening, Unconditional Love, Liberation, and Transformation

Second Edition
Revised

❁

by Scott Morrison

21st Century Renaissance Publishing

Copyright ✍ 1996, 1997, 2000

ISBN 1-882496-10-8

Philosophy/Psychology/Meditation

21st Century Renaissance

Web Site: http://www.openmindopenheart.org/

Email: staff@openmindopenheart.org

To Gangaji,
teacher, sister, friend,
river of freedom and joy,
brilliant ray of dawn in the Western sky,

as well as

Ananda
Arjuna Nick Ardagh
Cameron Spradling
Chahna Dumont
Glenn Francis
Hanuman
H.W.L. Poojaji
H. H. the Dalai Lama
Isaac Shapiro
Jiddu Krishnamurti
Ken Wilber
Ramana Maharshi
Stormy Knight
Thich Nhat Hanh
Toni Packer

and all who freely share the Truth
that can neither be written nor spoken.

And a Special Thank You

There are quite a few people, both named and unnamed, who contributed significantly to this work, and I would like to express deep gratitude and respect to all of them. And to the following small group of friends in particular, whose encouragement, love, and support were critical in making this possible: Laverne Griffith, Tom DeBerry, Nancy Chase, Glenn Francis, Cameron Spradling, Tom Ashley, Helga Umpierre, Richard Downs, Lida Torres, Shanti Ragyi, Yakeen Ragyi, Mary Axtmann, Lady Lee Andrews, Kirk Thompson, Melissa Simpson, Jim and Betty Caton, Elena Moore, Lytengale and Chad O'Shea, Mark King, Karen King, Jacque Patterson, Colleen Lyons, Lisa Saunders, Donna Kramer, Frances Milam, Christopher Schilling, Rob Rhodes, Mary Frances Myers, and dharma buddy Dick Grace.

Contents

Also by Scott Morrison

Books:

Intimate Awareness

Open and Innocent
The Gentle, Passionate Art of Not-Knowing

Audio Tapes:

*Enlightenment
Is Unconditional Intimacy with This Moment
*Liars Anonymous
*The Ecstasy of Not Being Anybody
*Just Give Up
*Jesus Was Not a Christian
and
Buddha Was Not a Buddhist
*The Gentle, Passionate Art of Not-Knowing
*There Is Only Now
*One Breath at a Time:
Serenity and Spiritual Awakening
especially for People in Recovery
*Love Exists Only on This Breath
*Spiritual Friendship & Intimate Community
*Waking Up Together
*Sexual Healing & Spiritual Awakening
*On the Brink of Total Freedom
*The Peace That Depends on Nothing

INTRODUCTION

The End of All Seeking

The Silence of Hurricanes

I've always loved hurricanes. The wilder, less predictable and more perilous, the better. Growing up in New Orleans, there was at least one, or the threat of one, every summer. It would begin with the weather bulletins interrupting "Life of Reilly" or "Father Knows Best," to announce that "a tropical disturbance, rapidly increasing in size and strength, seems to be moving in a northwesterly direction from its present location, 120 miles south/southeast of the U.S. Virgin Islands. Given present weather conditions, we think it may be heading this way. Small craft warnings will be issued from Galveston to Pensacola... "

And so it began. Slowly, surely, gathering momentum. A tropical storm. The Virgins, just south of Puerto Rico. Larger, stronger, 75 . . . 85 . . . 95 . . . with gusts of over 120 m.p.h.... a hurricane, perhaps a very dangerous one, still growing in size and speed as it moved into the warm waters of the Gulf of Mexico. Over the course of the next day or so, whole families at home, and everyone at the barber shop or beauty shop would suddenly stop talking to listen, one-pointedly, to the increasingly more frequent and serious reports as to the growing intensity, speed and direction of this massive, unknown force heading our way. Giving it a name at some point did little to diminish the mysterious excitement of the whole thing.

As it became apparent that this mighty tropical cyclone, which soon looked roughly like a humongously overweight tornado on the weather map (already several times the size of our entire city) was most likely coming ashore somewhere in the vicinity of the Mississippi Gulf Coast, a strange and miraculous shift would occur. As the skies darkened and the winds intensified, people began to move about with a definite sense of clarity and purpose, buying candles, flashlight batteries, canned goods, plywood and tape for their windows, contacting their families and loved ones, planning for the safety of people in their neighborhoods.

People who did not normally even recognize each other's existence would gently smile at one another on the street, in quiet acknowledgment that things were different now. It was as if some silent, secret directive clicked in with every human being alive, overriding all other concerns and states of mind. Without words, but very clearly, it said:

> "Immediately drop whatever you are
> thinking and doing. Pay very close
> attention to whatever is happening.
> Be ready to help, if needed."

In all of this, there was tremendous energy and focus, but no fear. That's right, nowhere in the midst of preparing for this overwhelming unknowable force, did there seem to be even the slightest trace of worry or anxiety.

Suddenly, there were no Republicans and no Democrats, no Christians, Jews, agnostics, or atheists, no gay people and no straight people, no blacks, whites, browns, reds, yellows, blue bloods or blue collars. No insiders or outsiders, no beautiful people and no ugly people. Everything was just what it was, nothing less, nothing more, without labels or divisions. Everywhere, there was just the energy of clear, undistracted attention, and unreserved, unconditional kindness and care for everyone.

The storms themselves were always astounding and thrilling. Being the wild bunch that we were, some of us would go out to the sea wall, where it was raining furiously and sideways, to lean forward into the wind, hoping for a gust powerful enough to lift us up off the ground! In the sixties and on into the seventies, we even had "hurricane parties," during which we would sit around and laugh and talk and sing and tell stories and generally act outrageous. A good part of the time friends and lovers would just sit quietly on the couch, holding each other and listening to the storm. The awesome power of nature, the freedom of the unknown, of innocence, of playfulness, of affection, of making love during the storm - all of it was *so alive*! Everything, yes, *everything*, was rich and wild and sweet and amazing, and even difficulty and danger and destruction, and the response to them,

were whole and complete, and in their own way, also
fascinating.

I've heard other people speak in a similar
way about earthquakes and tornadoes and
mudslides and blizzards, and even about the Great
Depression. What is possible in a storm or an
earthquake or any other kind of crisis, is possible at
any time, for virtually any human being who cares
enough to stop the world. If we abandon time, that
is, let go of obsessively thinking about ourselves,
about our past and our future, and give ourselves
in the purest way possible to simple, open awareness
and kindness, we set into motion something that is
without bounds or limits, something that
immediately and eventually touches everyone.
If you do and I do, it will affect those around us, who
in turn will affect others, and still others.

Who knows what is possible? An enlightened
city? A nation of mystics? Perhaps even an entire
humanity that excludes no one, awake and free.
This process has, in fact, begun in any number of
different places with a rapidly growing number of
people. Not hopefully or theoretically, but actually --

I've seen it, witnessed it in my travels through hundreds of different towns and cities over the past decade or so. It's also happening in the Caribbean, in Europe, Australia, Asia, and in Latin America. This last few years, letters of confirmation and encouragement, as well as inspired visitors, have arrived from France, Germany, Switzerland, Holland, Denmark, Spain, Great Britain, Israel, Saudi Arabia, South Africa, India, Nepal, Australia, Indonesia, Japan, Brazil, and Mexico. It cannot be owned or controlled by anyone, and it is occurring everywhere. How does it happen? It occurs only when you're ready, in a state of complete innocence, openness, and willingness, as is always the case in matters of the heart. Will there be critical mass? Who will be the hundredth monkey?

The Intimate Passion of This Moment

This book is not about anyone's ideas of perfection. It is not about any religious or moral or mental versions of spirituality. It is not about anything anyone is "supposed to be." This is a book about *loving without deliberation or hesitation*. It is a book about being alive - completely, absolutely, unconditionally *alive*. It is a book about happiness and the end of all seeking. It is a book about peace.

There is only now. Everything we call the "past" is *absolutely nothing but present memory*, and highly edited memory at that. Everything we call the "future" is absolutely nothing but fantasy and commentary, that is, *present memory recycled and rearranged*. If we continue to fantasize and pretend there is some other time or place to be, besides right here, right now, we are cruelly and pathologically deluding ourselves. *Now* is the only "time" we can ever be awake and free, honest, wise, intimate, or compassionate. Now is the only time we can ever love. Now is the only time we can ever be happy or at peace.

This work is offered as a clear, simple, and direct guide to Self-realization: that is, enlightenment, love, liberation, and transformation. Nothing herein is theoretical or speculative; it comes only from direct experience, and, as such, is completely verifiable. It is written as a practical guidebook for the individual who is seriously considering the possibility of total freedom.

There are three fundamental requirements for this work:

1. An unconditional commitment to unbiased observation and honest reflection.
2. An unconditional commitment to unbiased observation and honest reflection.
3. An unconditional commitment to support others in this process.

Further, it is useful to remember that this is intimate, investigative work, with no entangling alliances to any system of belief or authority. Let's be clear and honest from the very beginning: It is only love that paves the way, and it is only the truth that sets us free. All you really need is a completely open heart, and a completely open mind.

Basic Happiness and the Laws of Motive

This book is an invitation to happiness and
freedom. Some of this is ancient, some of
it contemporary, and some unique to the conditions
of our particular cultures and subcultures. No
matter what the source, history, or the context,
however, the aim and the focus here is upon offering
down-to-earth, cause-and-effect information about
how life works in as clear and as accessible a way as
possible, much of which is still, amazingly,
somewhat of a rarity in our times.

First and foremost, take your time with this!
It will not work if you rush through this, just trying
to accumulate information, memorizing ideas,
mastering the jargon, agreeing with this,
disagreeing with that. I strongly urge you do none
of that, but rather investigate directly to find out
for yourself. For the best results, take it slowly and
methodically, experimenting very honestly and
carefully as you proceed. For instance, if you read
something to the effect that greed is a form of
tension and distraction, which simply causes more

greed, tension and distraction, I suggest that you neither accept it nor reject it. Instead, carefully examine ways that you do, in fact, crave something, and see if it results in the experience of happiness and freedom, or worry, tension, frustration, and more craving. You may crave money or financial security. You may crave the attention or affection or approval of other people. You may crave sexual pleasure. You may crave religious prestige, spiritual recognition or experiences. Maybe all of the above. Maybe none of the above. Maybe something else. Just be objective. Honest investigation is not about who is right or wrong, good or bad, spiritual or not spiritual, better or lesser than the next person. It is simply about what the truth is. That's all.

What you will be exposed to in the following pages will give you very clear-cut choices, not all of them easy, but every one of them worth considering with very great care and sincerity. Again, it is not based on morality, religion, philosophy, or any set of socially sanctioned assumptions. (If we are going to honestly explore what is real and true, *we can't assume anything* in advance.) It is not designed to make you a "better person," although it would not be surprising if, at some point, someone you've known for a while might make some remark about how relaxed or warm or peaceful you seem these days. If you truly are interested in what it takes to be happy, not theoretically in some vague and distant future, but actually and immediately, then read on. This is a simple, practical and highly usable guidebook on *what is*. It's very honest and logical, and it works. Even if one were to choose to remain unhappy, worried, stressed, depressed, or angry, that person would at least know who is making the decisions. Finally, this is not a book about positivity overcoming negativity, and it is not a book about optimism overcoming pessimism. I hope that by now it is clear that this is a book about life and a book about reality. However, bear in mind that the truth is not in books, and it's not in the words. In order for this to work for you, you must open your heart and mind to discover what the words are pointing to. Deep in your own heart – this is where the truth really lives. Find it and give yourself to it. Give yourself to it completely and be happy. Nothing real is in the way.

14

BASIC HAPPINESS

How Life Works

How Life Works

What follows are both ancient and contemporary scientific and spiritual laws. As such, again, it is not in your interest to believe in them or blindly follow them, for in institutional settings and often in our own minds, they are sometimes misunderstood and manipulated for a wide variety of reasons that have nothing to do with the basic, down-to-earth, day-to-day functional wisdom upon which they are based.

Since they are completely verifiable, a much more intelligent and honest approach would be to simply experiment with them in your life, your work, your relationships, your sexuality, your financial affairs, your politics and so on, to find out not only *whether* they work, but exactly *how* they work.

The foundation of any serious spiritual life, indeed, any intelligent life at all, is *clarity of intention*. This means that we are willing to be completely clear and honest with ourselves as to what our motives and directions really are. It also means *purity* of intention, *integrity* of intention, and *sincerity* of intention. It means we are **undivided**. Implicit in this is the question, "Just how serious am I about this?" Are my intentions mixed? Am I being completely honest with myself as to what my dominant intentions really are? Am I willing to follow through on this question, no matter how challenging it may be? When push comes to shove, is the truth more important than anything else?

These are the kinds of questions that determine how real and how serious we are about spiritual awakening, love, and liberation. How we answer them, not just in words, but by being and doing, determines our success and our happiness.

Sense Happiness and Clarity of Motive

Everybody wants to be happy and at peace. The problem is that the vast, vast majority of us invest most of our attention, time, and energy on motives and activities that will not only inevitably frustrate any kind of ongoing serenity or happiness, but are also guaranteed to cause suffering. It is not because we, as a species, are masochistic or stupid, it is simply that we are ignorant. Ignorance, in this sense, simply boils down to a lack of a clear, functional understanding of how life works. So how *does* it work? Everyday wisdom begins with the **Law of Motive**, and this is how it goes:

> Happiness is not a so much matter of ***what*** you think, or *what* you say, or *what* you do; it's not even in *what happens to you*. But rather, it's ***how*** you think what you think, *how* you say what you say, *how* you do what you do, *how* you experience what you experience. In plain language, that means that whatever you think, say, do, or

experience, if you do so out of *awareness*, out of *kindness*, out of *compassion*, out of *honesty*, out of *insight* and *understanding*, out of *generosity*, the result, both immediately and down the road, will be one of joy, happiness, peace, freedom, and beauty, not only for you, but often those around you. If, on the other hand, you think, speak, act, or experience out self-centered motives such as greed, anger, control, competitiveness, dishonesty, denial, ignorance, or the intention to cause harm, the result, both immediately and down the road, will be one of confusion, suffering and ugliness. So, again, the **art of being happy,** joyous, free, and at peace is **not in the what**, it is **in the how**.

We've all heard it said that "The road to hell is paved with good intentions." However, this is not quite true. It might be more accurate to say, "The road to misery, that is, hell on earth, is paved with ignorance of what our intentions really are!" In other words, it may be easy for me to say that my motive is to be aware, to love, to be wise, and so on. However, if my actions reflect something entirely different, it may be useful for me to see if I have been deceiving myself as to what my dominant intentions really are. Upon honest reflection, I may find that some motives, which may only show themselves under special conditions, have more to do with me getting my way, getting what I think I want, or avoiding what I don't want at any given time.

Well, so what, you might say. Isn't trying to get what we want pretty much what everyone is doing? The answer to that question, I'm afraid, is an unfortunate yes. And the fact that this strategy has gone on unquestioned and unexamined, except in the most superficially moralistic way, is itself pretty amazing, given the fact that it doesn't work. Let's be very clear at this point: there is nothing particularly wrong with desire, with wanting something. Bodies have needs and wants. If you want to eat, and there is good food available, go ahead and eat. If you are tired and want to sleep, go ahead and lie down. If you want to make love with someone who wants to make love with you, and it won't cause any harm to anyone, then there is not a problem. The real problem arises, however, in *clinging to an object of desire*. What do we mean by clinging? When some memory or fantasy or idea of something you would like, something you want or think you need, becomes the dominant consideration, you restrict your awareness, and compare whoever or whatever is present unfavorably to the fantasy, to the object of mental desire. In other words, the thought becomes more important than the reality. From that point on, you are a slave to clinging and craving, and nothing can be seen clearly, directly, or honestly. Everything is edited or blocked, according to how it serves that desire. In this clinging and craving, there is no love and no joy and no freedom.

A similar kind of problem arises when we obsess on the memory of something that we perceive as hurtful or humiliating or threatening. To be aware of our feelings may be very useful, but if we nurse these memories, raging or worrying or wallowing in them over and over and over again, then we are simply rehearsing them, entrenching them, and ultimately, all we are really doing is denying ourselves, and possibly those around us, a great deal of goodness, beauty, happiness, and peace. So what to do? When we find ourselves doing that, the only way to healing and freedom is forgiving and letting go.

But what about being proactive? Is there any way keep it from getting to this point? Here is where it is very important to be very specific and very honest with ourselves as to what our intentions and motives actually are. Spelling it out:

The motive to *love,* and the tendency to *crave, cling,* or *use people* are two radically different and unrelated approaches to living.

The motive to *be generous,* to *give* and to *share,* and the *ambition to acquire, possess,* and *control* are two radically different and unrelated approaches to living.

The motive to *include and be kind*, and the *tendency to compete, undermine, gossip, lash out, attack, hate, exclude, speak,* or *act out of a desire to hurt*, are two radically different and unrelated approaches to living. The motive to *understand*, to *think, see, hear, speak, and act honestly and wisely* and the *tendency to ignore, deny, hide, deceive, and mislead oneself and others* are two radically different and unrelated approaches to living.

So why spell out what, for many, is so obvious? In the first place, even though most of us give lip service to a great deal of what is above, most of us don't take it all that seriously when it comes into conflict with our desire to have things go our way. Second, in everyday, functional terms, very few people are truly aware of the direct and easily verifiable relationship between motive and happiness to any significant degree. This is why there is so much suffering in the world. To the vast majority, happiness has more to do with physical or mental circumstances, or how the body feels, or what the dominant emotion happens to be at any given moment. What most people don't realize is that motives, tendencies, habits, and intentions are *choices*, not always easy choices, but ones with very definite results and consequences.

So, the invitation here is to check it out for yourself and be very honest with yourself as to what your real motives are, and take careful note of the quality of the experience. Again:

-On the one hand, paying attention, loving, caring, giving, sharing, understanding, including, and living honestly, compassionately, and wisely create the conditions for great happiness and beauty on all levels, most obviously on the level of sense happiness.

-On the other, clinging, craving, using, acquiring, possessing, attempting to control, competing, undermining, gossiping, attacking, lashing out, hating, excluding, and acting out of the intention to harm, create the conditions for great suffering, ugliness, and misery, particularly on the level of sense happiness.

What, exactly, do we mean by sense happiness? Sense happiness includes simply being able to enjoy and take pleasure in the rich and beautiful experiences of the senses: sights, sounds, smells, tastes, feelings, emotions, and even mental sensations.

We do not necessarily get to choose, and certainly do not control, our circumstances (even though we may influence them.) We do, however, have immediate and absolute choice over our motives. In order for us to exercise this choice, there must be uncompromising self-awareness and self-honesty. So happiness, even on the level of sense pleasure, is a choice. How that happiness unfolds is not up to us. (Again, we don't control it.) But the fact that it is possible, and entirely workable, is easily verifiable.

Stop, at this point, begin experimenting and observing to find out. How do I know these things to be true? From my own life and the lives of many friends. Find if it is true for yours. Reflect and experiment, for example, with *the how* (the motive, as opposed *to the what*) of thought, speech, and action, that is tied to clinging, craving, and using. How does it feel? There may be the initial pleasure and excitement of fantasizing and thinking about getting something we want. But stay with it. Does it not eventually become a kind of tension? Keep on observing to see how it all unfolds, without judgment or condemnation, but rather with simple curiosity? How does it really work? Let the truth of it really sink in. "Getting as much of as many things as I want for me" is pretty much the given strategy for happiness in our time. So let's be very scientific and very honest here: How does it *really* feel when we use somebody, when we make him or her an object of pleasure or financial or emotional security? How do we feel, during and afterwards? What happens to the relationship, the friendship, and the easiness of being together? Even sex, do we truly enjoy it in a deep and satisfying way? What happens when we begin to think of someone as a source of income, or prestige, as an identification with beauty or power? What happens when we try to own or control that person, or when we begin to take them for granted? No matter how subtle, that is a decision. How does it feel to be around that person once that decision is made? We may sometimes get what we want, but how much and how deeply and for how long do we really enjoy it?

Continue the experiment: when sexual involvement is an expression of love, affection, intimacy, generosity and gratitude, how does *that* feel? During and afterward? When there is no using, and therefore no separation, who is the giver, and who is the receiver?

When you approach your financial affairs with a sense of generosity, creating situations where everybody is served, where everybody wins: your employer, your employees, your colleagues, your customers, your patients, your students, your clients, how does that feel? Notice what a far cry it is from competition, usury, and accumulation. Notice what a radical difference there is when you include instead of compete or exclude.

Again, all of this may seem obvious to many of us, but the reason that we rarely, if ever, actually live in this way is that we do not have a clear, everyday, functional understanding that it is our choice of these intentions that determines whether we actually enjoy our lives. So don't stop here--keep experimenting. There is a great deal at stake. Find out, and begin making serious choices. As you do this, notice how it affects the quality of your life.

Beyond Sense Happiness

Sense happiness and sense pleasures can be wonderful and very sweet. They can be fun. Every once in a while, they can be exquisite. They are good for what they are, but they have one major drawback, in that they are short-lived; they are temporary. We want them to last, we hope against hope, but we can't seem to hold onto them. They appear; then they disappear. They cannot do otherwise: It's their nature. So what else is there?

Clarity of Mind

An even deeper and more sustained level of
happiness has to do with clarity and purity of mind,
that is, a mind that is not distracted by conflict and
disturbance. Other common words for it are
concentration, absorption and *samadhi*. What this
means is cultivating and exploring the pleasure,
beauty, and power of deep, sustained, one-pointed
attention. Absorption is a skill, a challenging but
learnable one, and it requires your full attention, in
the same way that learning mathematical or musical
or athletic skills do. More specifically, it requires
single-minded *precision* and *continuity*. The good
news is that as you learn how to give yourself to it,
you begin to notice increasingly pleasant sensations
arising. Beyond a certain point, it is self-reinforcing,
and you will begin to experience periods of sustained
bliss.

To begin, you must first choose an object of
concentration that you are willing to stay with,
generally some physical sensation or mind-body
state. It will work with just about anything, but

certain objects of attention seem to work better than others, depending on the person. You can choose the sensation of breathing, with your body and especially your abdomen relaxed, and your attention focused at belly level, on the rising and falling of inhalation and exhalation. (An alternative is to focus on the sensation of breathing just inside of your nostrils.) Or you can choose some other sensation: a flower, a candle flame, a picture of someone you love and admire, a sound, a chant, a piece of music, or an internal sound, such as a mantra. It can be love, generosity, understanding, compassion, or peace. One that has worked exceptionally well for me is focusing on the joy, happiness, and peace of loving kindness for all of us everywhere.

There are a number of excellent books on the various techniques, skillful means and methods, particularly those by Thich Nhat Hanh, Jack Kornfield, Pema Chodron, Gunaratana Mahathera, and Stephen Levine, but the fundamentals for all of them are pretty much the same. Anything that does not tend to generate very much additional thought, in other words, anything that is enjoyable paying attention to that you are not likely to get into some kind of mental discussion or conflict over should work fine. Bear in mind that what you are developing is not some special relationship with the object, but rather a very intimate, subtle, even microscopic investigation of the intense beauty and ecstatic pleasure of awareness itself. This is a very, very important point. To pursue one of these methods, it may be helpful to find a good teacher or friend whose guidance you can trust and a method that works, and give it everything you've got. You won't be disappointed.

Once you have begun to discover the elegant, tender, and subtle beauty of one-pointed consciousness, you may find your want to take this further, perhaps much, much further . . . . Why? Because as sweet as it is, absorption, also, is temporary. It, too, is conditional. So, is there anything that is not???

Clarity of View

If you are open and honest, inquisitive and courageous enough, you will realize that everything you thought you knew about your life, about the world, about everything in the world, about spirituality, about love, about God, about enlightenment, about consciousness itself, has been based on the beliefs, opinions, and assumptions of other people, and what you *think* about those beliefs and assumptions. In other words, everything you think you know is *all based on memory and thought.* When you realize that even the most respected and authoritative sources don't really know either, you may find yourself teetering on the brink of something both terrifying and thrilling.

The massive shock of realizing that you know absolutely nothing about yourself, and you know absolutely nothing about the universe reveals a profound intimacy and wonder that you could not even begin to put into words. It is an immediate, absolute intimacy with *what is* and with *all that is.*

When you discover it, you realize that this is not some kind of altered state, but simply *how it is*. You will also realize that you **are** this intimacy. There is literally nothing else left to do. Just let it have its way with everything. It already *is* everything. It is the end of all seeking. I strongly urge you not to think of it as enlightenment or *kensho* or *moksha* or any other label. In fact, I suggest you not think about it at all, but rather, simply give yourself to it, unconditionally. In other words, **go ahead and be what you already are.**

What follows are various expressions of This, a small host of ways of saying what cannot be said. Whether you finish all of them or not is unimportant. What *is* important, however, is that whatever you do read, you read *very slowly and with great care*, with your heart and mind completely open. If you do, you may come upon something infinitely larger, smaller, higher, wider, deeper, sweeter and more precious than anything you ever dared hope for. (It could be this very instant, if you're ready.)

It has no name. It is everywhere and It is the very core of your being. It is purer than purity itself, and there is nowhere it cannot be found. Once you do discover It, you will no longer be able to say whether you found It or It found you. And you will no longer have anything to say about you at all.

The Bliss of Surrender

It's fairly simple and straightforward:
If you want to be happy,
If you want to realize complete freedom,
You just give up everything for love.
No conditions, no reservations.

Everything means everything:
Give your arms and legs,
your hands, and your feet,
your head, your hair, and your face,
your appearance,
your eyes, your ears, your tongue,
your heart, your brain, your genitals,

Your circumstances, your relationships,
your money, your power,
your pleasure, your pain,
your pretenses of inferiority and superiority,

Everything you like,

everything you don't like,

Your whole life, and everything in it,

Everything you see, hear, smell, taste,

touch, feel, and think.

Let it all be the expression

and the experience of love,

of affection, compassion, and joy,

of friendliness, honesty, care, and wisdom.

The only time you can do that is now.

If you want to be happy, that is.

What, then, is Love?

Then what, exactly, is love? Like awareness, it is impossible to put into words exactly what love is. Love is a lot bigger and infinitely more fluid than words or concepts or the mind process that creates and reinforces them. However, most people recognize love when it is present, and a good rule of thumb is that ***true love*** *always tastes like, and always feels like,* ***freedom and joy***. If it feels tense, restrictive, or troubling in any way, then it's not love; it's something else masquerading as love.

True love is, in fact, what you discover you *are*, the instant you cease to be preoccupied with yourself as a separate entity with its endless ambitions, problems and worries. Then you will discover that your true nature is love, and that it requires no belief or effort whatsoever. Furthermore, if you give yourself to That, you will realize complete freedom and happiness, and your struggles with the world will come to an end, if that is what you truly want.

Be *Absolutely* Selfish!

So, in a sense, the problem has not been that we have been *too selfish*, it has been that *we have not been selfish enough*. We have been selfish in a narrow, naive, clumsy, poorly thought-out way. Why not be so selfish that we include *all* of what we are?

Why not give ourselves to the joy, happiness, peace, and freedom from suffering of *everyone everywhere?* Why not indulge in affection and take joy in everything? Think about it. Nothing real is stopping you.

What Is Enlightenment?

It is dusk, and the sounds of the rain forest,
the many frogs and night birds and insects
beginning to talk to each other, all of it is slowly
becoming delightfully noisy. The heat and
brightness of the day is giving way to a soft blue-
purplish-gray, which is bathing everything in its
slightly humid coolness. The breath rises and falls
in a long, steady rhythm, and the muscles and joints
pulsate with tired, good-achy sensations from the
day's hiking. There is a distant sputtering of a truck
coming up the mountain from the village below,
where there are also traces of music and laughter.
All of this, as well as the city, a sparkling field of
diamonds to the far west, and the ocean beyond, is
engulfed in a vast and endless silence.

Most everyone is sitting still, some relaxed, a
few others occasionally looking around expectantly,
perhaps wondering what is appropriate. A little girl,
around eight or ten, sitting with her mother, looks
up sheepishly. We smile at each other. A young
man, dressed in white, slender and earnest, listens

carefully to what is being said as he prepares himself to speak.

Question: *I liked what you said about awareness and wisdom, but the question, for me at least, goes to the heart of the matter. Are you enlightened? What is enlightenment? Forgive me for being blunt and skeptical, but I hear a lot of people talking about it, some implying that they are, or that they know of someone who is, generally their teacher, but I'm not convinced they know what they are talking about.*

There is nothing wrong with healthy skepticism, or speaking frankly, for that matter. To suspend everyone's prior assumptions, including yours and mine, is to be open to that which is true, that which is new and fresh.

These questions you are asking about whatever you may imagine enlightenment to be, however, are not about me, they are about you, are they not? Rather than giving ourselves over to a whole entourage of beliefs and opinions, let's take a look at what is implied by the question. Maybe you have heard certain things about this "enlightened teacher" or that, this Buddhist or Hindu or yogic group or that, radical dharma or traditional sitting or *koan* practice or whatever. So, depending on what you think about what you've read or heard, whether you were inspired or encouraged or validated or offended, you show up at a gathering to get some kind of impression which will confirm, or possibly contradict, your hopes or suspicions. So, you like this person in the front of the room--she, or he, is friendly, or speaks with great power or charisma, so you decide well, maybe, and you sign up to attend the next satsang or sesshin or retreat or maybe join the sangha or group and so on. Or perhaps there is something disturbing about this person, something in his or her eyes or tone of voice or body language, then it's on to the next teacher. Why not go, as you say, to the very heart of your second question?

I don't want to put words in your mouth, but when you ask, "What is enlightenment?" I think you are really asking whether such a thing is possible for you. Is that true?

Yes.

The definition is simple enough, but the real question is whether you are willing to find out, what it is, not according to someone else, not according to the concept or the philosophy, but for yourself, in a direct and immediate way that puts an end to all questions.

To be enlightened is to be unconditionally intimate with this moment. There is no other time or place to give yourself, totally, to *all that is*. Everything else about spiritual experiences and transformation is just memory, speculation and fantasy, is it not? So why not put preconceived notions and images of enlightenment, liberation, realization, *satori*, *moksha*, *kensho*, *nirvana*, and so on aside, and see what is possible right now?

The most important question is, are you willing to give up on any desire to get or become or defend anything at all, and are you willing to do that completely? Are you really willing to give up on self-centered strategies that haven't ever worked anyway? If you are not, then it's important to be honest about it, so that you are not pretending to be interested when in fact you are infatuated with something else, whether it is approval, admiration, affection, sex, money, power, some kind of personal recognition or security or gratification, some spiritual experience or status, escape, some project you hope will lead you to happiness, or whatever.

Your question, then, if it is serious, is about something much more subtle than all of that, and demands an attention that is undivided and undistracted in even the slightest way. If you are willing, completely willing, to let go of everything you think of as "your self" and "your life," to bring it all to an absolute STOP, right now, then something profoundly sensitive and beautiful will be free to reveal itself. In this revelation, all questions may be dissolved into an ocean of tenderness and joy and gratitude. Why not be absolutely still, and find out, now, if that is so?

Two Lovers

Each one of us has a choice
between two lovers.
One is alive, one is not.

One is predictably shallow, cruel and boring,
sadistic and gnawingly monotonous.
The other is completely insecure,
unknown and unknowable.

One seems to keep you hoping and expectant,
annoyed, irritated, and defensive.
The other always surprises you,
in ways you can never really pin down.

One promises you pleasure, but will always
betray you and leave you disappointed.
The other moves you deeply,
and is never even a breath away.

One promises you relief,
but knows nothing of serenity.
The other promises nothing,
but is whole and complete,
and nothing is lacking in the silence.

One is your servant, but never listens to you.
The other is your teacher,
and illuminates the world.

One brings sorrow, loneliness, and self-loathing.
The other embraces all that you are
with complete understanding.

One leaves you longing, worried and tired.
The other leaves you nothing,
yet you are endlessly fulfilled.

One lives in a place called Thought,
obsessive and craving.
The other lives nowhere and everywhere,
has no name or address.
Yet you always know where to look.

The domain of thought is only the Known,
restricted to memory and fantasyizing,
complaining, and criticizing,
denying and rationalizing,
endlessly , hopefully, hopelessly,
bound to times past and future
and a present you can't get to.

The Unknown is everywhere
and everything
and then some.
.

Throughout your life you have come to know
the first one very well, restless and bored,
always tired, sleeping on the floor.
The other is new, yet strangely familiar,
somehow mysteriously intimate.

Finally!
The clock has stopped,
and time has run out.

Who will it be?

The only One who can touch you
can be touched by nothing,
and comes with no guarantees.
And the price? Is your life.

Does that seem too much
for what you've been looking for
all these many years?
You must finally choose,
or the other wins by default.

Love Does Not Exist in Time

Question: *I know that time is an illusion, but what about planning? Is there room in this for planning for the future?*

There is nothing wrong with using the holographic and conceptual capabilities of memory and fantasy to work creatively with each other and our environment. Using those capabilities, we may arrange to have lunch together, plan a vacation, build a home, educate a child, publish radical dharma on the internet, or any number of other things. The problem arises when we confuse that mechanism, that creative prediction system, that set of possibilities, which is made entirely of thought, with something infinitely larger, that is, the vast, dynamic, constantly interacting and transforming reality of which thought is only a minuscule and very limited model. In truth, there is no "future." That is just a word we use to refer to fantasizing about how it might be or how we want it to be or how we are afraid it might be. What we imagine to be the "future" is completely unknown. All we can do is predict, and then see what happens. But the reality is what happens, not the prediction.

If you completely abandon your compulsive preoccupation with your mental/emotional versions of yourself, with their endless ambitions and the constant flow of problems that arise because of them, it's an absolute shock! You will find that they were completely fictitious--they never existed in the first place. They were just part of some bad movie you saw at some point, continued to replay, and came to believe in. That may be an especially rude shock if they have been the center of your attention, as they have for practically everybody, all of your life, for ten, twenty, maybe fifty years or more. But, better late than never. (It's not wasted, at any rate, for you will be potentially of great help to anyone else who is trying to find their way out of all this culturally created confusion.)

If you actually do stop obsessing in this way, you will discover the sweet, wonderful, blessed truth: That your true nature is love. You will realize that beneath the surface of all of your competing and struggling and defensiveness, there has been nothing but love all along. Then the ecstatic bliss that is this realization will fill the whole universe.

This Is Everything

Question: *Sometimes I think I make it much too complex; my mind just goes on and on. Do you think there is hope for someone like me?*

It's not a matter of hope. It's a matter of facing reality. Just keep it simple. It all comes down to this:

Stop thinking you have time,
that you can somehow put it off until later.
You can do anything you like, of course,
but the fact remains that you are either willing to
investigate and embrace the truth at any cost, right
now, or you are going in the opposite
direction,solidifying your habit of avoiding, escaping,
and denying it.

So:

This is it. This is everything.

This, right here, right now, is your whole life.

Whatever you are doing, saying,

thinking, being,

right now,

is your whole life.

This is not only your best shot,

it's the only one you know you've got.

Love, or hate,

Be wise, or be petty.

Be kind, or be cruel.

Open your heart,

or keep it blocked and hidden away.

Open your mind,

or stay locked in on fixed views.

Be honest with yourself,

or hold on to prior opinions,

pretend to be superior or inferior,

or pretend nothing at all.

Embrace the freshness and newness of life:

pain, pleasure, difficulty, easiness, unknown
-- all of it, or try to run away
from your fear of taking a risk.

Be awake and free, or pretend you're not,
and that you're not responsible
for the state of your life.

Give it everything you've got,
or ignore the possibilities.

Live it, or try to avoid it.
It's completely up to you.

Because this is it.
This is everything.

Simpler Still

Question: *I know this sounds ridiculous, but I keep on forgetting and getting lost in internal debate and distraction. I'm still not sure what to do.*

Relax.
Smile (if you like).
Pay attention.
Be honest.
Be wise.
Be kind.
Don't cause any harm.
Stop trying to hold onto things.

In general, the simpler, the better.
So if that's still too complicated,
then just pay attention, be honest,
and don't cause any harm.

Open Your Mind

The problem is not with your heart. If you completely open your mind, you will discover your heart has always been open. It only appears to be closed, hesitant, or confused when you mistake what you think about love for love itself.

Just Stop Lying

The Way of Realization is not difficult. All you have to do is open your eyes! If you allow yourself to see things as they actually are, without confusing yourself with prior opinions, everything will be clear and freedom will be everywhere.

You just have to laugh at what liars we've all been!

Does Enlightenment Really Take Time?

There is only now.
The full realization of boundless freedom
and infinite peace,
of wisdom, love and compassion,
is simply a completely open heart
and a completely open mind.
Right here, right now.

Wake up!
Come totally and immediately,
once and for all,
to terms with the simple fact that
you know absolutely nothing about yourself,
and you know absolutely nothing
about the universe.

There is literally nothing else to do.

The Ugliest Man I Ever Saw

Question: *When I hear you talk about total surrender and having nothing to lose, it scares me. I want to let go, but for some reason, I can't. I guess I'm afraid it will not be as exciting. (He went on to talk in great length about his sex life, and how there are spiritual paths to enlightenment based on sexual ecstasy, and how he is afraid he will have to give that up.)*

It's not that you can't let go -- it's that you won't. That's a pivotal discovery, that is, realizing that it is an absolute and immediate choice, and you are choosing, this very moment, out of ignorance, not to let go. That doesn't make you a bad person, but it's important to be honest. Ignorance is simply a lack of clear and complete understanding. You are not willing to let go because you are afraid you will have to give up something central to your identity. That is true. You will. You will have to give up boredom. You will have to give up cynicism. You will have to give up limitation and resentment. You will have to give up being hopeful and unfulfilled and disappointed. You will have to give up thinking of yourself as a victim and blaming other people.

Furthermore, after listening to you talk about your sex life, two things are apparent: One is that whatever sexual experiences you are having, you are not truly there for them, you are not giving yourself to them, you are not really enjoying them. Please, stay with me on this--it's important! The second is that whatever you are calling your sex life is tied up almost entirely in *thinking about sex*--longing, craving, or clinging to some memory or fantasy of what happened, or might happen, or what you saw in a movie or a commercial or whatever. What you are afraid of giving up is *your fictitious sex life, your mental sex life*. You may get yourself off as part of it, or even find a willing partner, and so there is maybe the pleasure of that, but if you continue to hold back, as if it were some kind of competition or manipulation, ultimately what good is it? Even if you find other people who are willing to cooperate, do you honestly think you are going to respect and enjoy a predictable lover? Have you ever? That's not passion, it's usury. If your whole approach to it is one of competing, negotiating, and holding back, that is, trying to own and control and use and eventually get rid of people as part of some fantasy-based strategy, you will continue to be frustrated, expectant, isolated, lonely, and all of the rest of it.

I'm not saying any of this to embarrass you-- many people, men and women, often surreptitiously, approach life this way. If it's not about sex, it's about money, power, prestige or some other object they imagine will bring happiness and security. Many even use their "spiritual path" that way. The important thing, however, is to face it squarely, honestly, stoically, and with great courage. You are *not living your life, you are fantasizing about living your life.* That's why, in spite of your insistence to the contrary, it's ultimately boring. It's dull. It's stupid. It's half dead. And in spite of the brief and limited gratification you may experience, there's a very good chance you secretly despise the whole thing. It shows all over your face.

This is because the memory/fantasy function, in spite of its enormous creative potential, is for most of us repetitious and unsatisfying, simply because we try to use it to replace the other 99.9% of reality that we are ignoring and avoiding. There is just no way mental life can match real life. Reality is vast and constantly interacting and changing and unknown and unpredictable. It is wondrous and mysterious and continuously amazing. If it seems like a risk, it's because you are still trying to protect something, still trying to manipulate things. So what you are afraid of giving up is a life of hopefulness and boredom and predictability, a life that you are still hoping you can control. But where there is predictability and control, or at least the appearance of it, there is no love and no joy and no happiness and no freedom. That is a simple fact.

So again consider, really, what have you got to lose? In your fantasy spiritual life, you are afraid no one will want to sleep with you or marry you, but in real life, it may actually be quite a bit different. Sometimes it seems like *everyone* wants to marry you and sleep with you and never let you go. How to respond consciously and compassionately in the face of that, now that's a *real* problem! I'm exaggerating, of course, but sometimes it seems that way. You are afraid no one will love you, but if you give yourself to love, completely and unconditionally, I suspect you will be very much surprised and overwhelmed with love and gratitude.

Once I met a Tibetan lama in the Rocky Mountains, and he gave a simple talk on awareness and kindness. Very simple, no big deal. He was, by his physical features, arguably the ugliest man I had ever seen. There was, however, beyond any doubt, a warmth in his eyes and throughout his whole being that was so powerful that all of us fell completely in love with him in just a matter of minutes. I think any of us would have gone just about anywhere to be with him. But he was returning to India, going back to his monastery, so that was that.

The point is, nowhere was there the slightest trace that he wanted anything from any of us. He was just absolutely, utterly, unconditionally kind. The possibility of holding back simply was not in him, and it was one of the most beautiful things I have ever seen. To be that way is a choice. It is perpetual and irreversible surrender. It is total willingness. Again, what have you really got to lose?

Let Your Heart Be Torn Open

Question: *What do you do when someone you trusted betrays that trust?*

Most of us will to try to escape, or go into denial or some kind of defense at the slightest sign of heartbreak. We will do just about anything to avoid getting hurt. We will try to avoid the pain with alcohol, drugs, food, entertainment, gossip, or any number of temporary escapes. We will lash out in anger, judgment, blaming, rationalization, justification, and hatred in an effort to get back at or get rid of the offending or rejecting party. What we forget in all of this is that *everyone's heart is broken*. Everybody hurts. In light of that simple fact, who did what to whom is suddenly unimportant.

Instead, boldly face your fear of heartbreak, put-down, humiliation, or rejection. Letting go of whatever you were afraid you wouldn't get or might lose, let your heart be ripped wide open. If you are courageous enough and honest enough to face the most painful hurt completely undefended, to let the most tender part of yourself be exposed to the cruelest and worst and most excruciating circumstances, you will discover an absolute miracle! Your heart is infinitely larger than you realized! It is big enough to contain all pain and all pleasure, all people, places, things, and circumstances. And there you will be, unafraid and in love with everybody and everything.

How Delusion Works

Question: *Why do we keep on falling prey to delusion,
to the mental version of life you speak of? There is a
situation involving another person that I can't seem
to let go of. You indicated something to the effect that
we are confused by the way the mind replays visual
memory. What did you mean by that?*

We continue to get caught because we have
not examined closely enough the nature of obsessive
thought and memory. In order to do that, we have to
bring up a thought we typically get entangled with
so as to catch ourselves in the act of identifying with
it in order to see how it works, and whether it is an
accurate representation of reality.

In part, it has to do with how the eyes focus
on an object, and then how the brain plays it back
later as memory or fantasy. For instance, let's say
you have an angry memory, involving some person
you met recently. Perhaps that person seemed to
offend you in some way. When you picture that
person, you pull up a disdainful expression on that

person's face. Mistaking the image remembered for the real person is where we get confused, and it is in part because we do not notice what happens when the eyes focus on an object.

When you look at a person's face, in order to see it clearly, you must focus on the area around the eyes or smile or whatever has attracted your attention. What that does, in effect, is take the rest of their body, as well as their surroundings, out of focus, so that it comes off as a kind of bland or meaningless background. Now, when you close your eyes and produce an after-image, the face may still be somewhat clear, but the background will be unfocused or murky, and if you play it back in memory later, or spin some kind of fantasy off of that memory, the greater context in which it occurs is even less noticeable. What's more, in reality, a person's face, eyes, emotions, and expressions are constantly changing, but little or none of that is recorded into the long-term memory of the event.

What this process does is create the impression that faces, or heads, or even bodies, are suspended in space, unchanging, repetitious, and not really connected to anything. What's more, when the image evokes some strong physical or emotional memory-response in your body, it is thereby anchored to and powerfully associated with a host of other emotional-memory story lines. So the static, offending picture of the person *feels real*, because the feeling is so strong, carrying with it the emotional baggage of all of the other associated memories.

So, again, if you watch the whole process carefully, you will notice that what is created in memory is not a living, breathing, feeling human being who is constantly reacting to a host of different people, feelings and changing circumstances, internal and external, but an isolated, static picture, frozen in time, associated, often subtly and automatically, with perhaps many other isolated, static memories of other people, all of the above anchored with a pattern of related feelings and muscular contractions. Remember that a memory is a whole system-process of mental and physical reactions and sensations that has a strong tendency to repeat itself. Each time it is repeated, the threshold is lowered. Because of the physical-emotional anchors (adrenaline, endorphins, serotonin, the biogenic amine system, etc.), it may "feel" very real and believable, even if it is grossly incomplete and totally misleading. And if it is believed, it becomes a habitual source of a chemical cocktail that brings feelings of dependability and security, sometimes even pleasure, even if the memory itself is unpleasant. If you do examine very closely and carefully to see how it works, as it is working, you will realize the memory-image or fantasy has very little to do with the real person in the whole complex, intricate, continuously changing context of their real life.

Auditory memory and mental commentary, with recorded sound bites, tones of voice, associated memories and so on, function in a similar way, and often just as convincingly.

It may come as quite a shock to discover what is played back in thought is nothing but a tiny and misleading fragment, because just about everyone is so thoroughly convinced that whatever they think about people, places, things, events and so forth, is an accurate representation of how it was and how it is. It may also be quite a disappointment as well, because if you continue the investigation, you also realize that the script of life isn't written around whatever you want or don't want, what you like or dislike. It's much bigger than that, and it exposes all hopes and attempts to own or control or get rid of anyone or anything as ludicrous, and in reality, a kind of self-torture.

However, if you truly let all of the implications of this sink in, it's a relief! On some level, you knew it wasn't real, and now you don't have to continue the charade. You are free to be completely and wholeheartedly involved with life as it actually is, which is not only much more workable, but infinitely more interesting.

The Appearance of a Separate Self

It is the replaying of variations of your "self image," along with commentaries on any given experience in what sounds more or less like your own voice that give you the impression of a "separate self." If you look and listen very closely, however, you will see that that "self" is nothing but a sound and light show, constructed out of memory/fantasy, and anchored with muscular contractions and other feelings in your body. Furthermore, if you look a little deeper, you will see that none of those self images look entirely like you. They are, instead, a morphing of some memory of yourself in the mirror or a photograph with the memory of whomever you were modeling yourself after at the time. So, it sort of looks like you, but it sort of looks like your father, or your mother, or your neurotic uncle, or somebody that you admired in high school or in a movie. That is why most of your self-images, if they look very much like you at all, tend to look like you at a much earlier age.

The same is true of mental commentary: The thought or opinion sort of sounds like you, but it also sort of sounds like someone else, based on whose voice was used in the original role model. All of this means that whoever you think you are is a construct made entirely of a very limited range of static, repetitious pictures and words, and in no way takes into account the infinite number of other things that make up you and your life.

Nor does it take into account that "who you are" includes everything it experiences, all of it in constant interaction and transformation and never staying the same from one moment to the next. Take just a few moments, if you will, to let that really sink in. If you do, with great diligence and care, it will shock your whole system awake. Don't take my word for it. Find out for yourself.

There Is Nothing Wrong

Question: *I know that what I am looking for I already am. I realize that awareness is always present and that I am that awareness. Yet seeking continues. How can it come to a stop? Or is it endless?*

Seeking is based on the idea that something is wrong -- something is wrong with you, something is wrong with your life, something is wrong with the world, and so on. We learn this at a very early age, and continue to imagine it to be so over and over and over again, in an endless number of settings, constantly trying to compensate for it. Question to the core this fundamental assumption: that there is a separate "you," as pictured or heard or fantasized or remembered in your mind, and that "he" needs to be improved, because he is somehow incomplete or unacceptable.

What is simply is. I don't see a shred of real evidence anywhere to support the idea that anything is wrong--with "you" or "me" or anybody or anything else. Of course, there are many things we may find difficult or that we don't like or wish to change, but that doesn't prove anything is wrong -- it just means we don't like them.

If you are willing to accept yourself and your life so thoroughly, such that "you" are no longer an issue, all seeking, all searching, all longing will cease. (And even if it arises again, it will be seen for the sham that it is.)

THE CORRUPTION OF INSIGHT

A Slap in the Face of the Buddha

The Corruption of Insight
A Slap in the Face of the Buddha

To be sure, we all have a great deal we can
learn from each other. However, the process of
subtle identification, arrogance and self-deception in
the spiritual arena is perhaps the most damaging of
all illusions. I am a Buddhist, or a Yogi, or a Pagan,
or a student of the Fourth Way or the Kabalah or
some other mystical or eclectic school, and I imagine
that Christians are at least somewhat deluded. Or I
am a Christian, perhaps a Catholic, or a Baptist or a
Mormon, or a *Course in Miracles* student, or a
Muslim, or a Jew, and maintain some pretense that
my version of "God" or "Love" is somehow more
genuine than "theirs."

But in fact, when we justify it with "Jesus
said so-and-so," or "The Buddha taught thus-and-
such," we might ask ourselves, "How would I know,
and why am I repeating this?" If we face it
sincerely, it is hard to avoid the discovery that all we
are doing is trying to bolster our own opinions and
their connected feelings, perhaps seeking to be tied

in with some long-lived tradition or powerful authority figure(s) established and fortified by our own conditioning. So we each have our private and group stories about things, and continue to surreptitiously elevate ourselves and put each other down.

But in fact, there is no private liberation or salvation. (Where is the "one separate" from the rest, to be saved or liberated, except in some mental fiction?) Of utmost importance, finally, is putting an end to this devious and hurtful process of "spiritual ego," of imagining there's some kind of competition, and that there's someone who has to defend his or her particular spiritual turf against others. If you stop using your transient body or your thoughts or feelings as points of reference, it will be obvious that there is no "someone" and there are no "others." That whole thing is a paranoid fantasy, a pathological delusion, in this case in the name of whatever religion or spiritual path to which we happen to subscribe. So let's call a spade a spade: God, the Absolute, does not belong to anyone, nor to any particular group. (So why pay homage to a limited god?)

Furthermore, enlightenment, liberation, Self-realization, do not belong to anyone either. (In fact, everything belongs to realization. So why pay homage to a limited enlightenment?) Although it may seem to occur in association with some context-- Buddhist, Christian, Yogic, Sufi, Hindu, Fourth Way, Muslim, Taoist, Jewish, Wiccan, 12-Step work, shamanistic, agnostic, scientific and so on, Spiritual Awakening, the Realization of Emptiness, the Tao, cannot be owned. How could That which is infinite be possessed by any religion, tradition, path, lineage, teacher, or hierarchy, all of which are limited? Is God a Christian, or a Jew, or a Muslim? Is enlightenment the property of Buddhists or yogis or Hindus? How could That which is formless be made to con-form to any set of assumptions about liberation, past or future? (If you still find yourself resisting that possibility, you might ask yourself how you would know, one way or the other, and what motives are tied up in thinking about it in any specified way, for or against. Why maintain beliefs or disbeliefs at all?) Is truth really a matter of subjective opinion? Is not truth, if that word means anything at all, an ongoing process of careful observation and uncompromising, undefended honesty?

It's time we stop pretending, subtly or overtly, that our particular group is superior in some way. That's a hidden way of saying, "I'm superior," (and therefore not inferior). Let's bring our woundedness, our childhood fears and hurts of inferiority, covered over by the pretense of individual or collective superiority, to a total and absolute halt. Completely. Now. If there are tears to be shed, then let's shed them together, and for each other. And let those tears of shame be tears of relief, tears of joy, in finally putting down this burden of trying to defend and justify what we have imagined ourselves to be. What doesn't exist in the first place doesn't need to be defended. It never did.

Particularly in recent years, many of us have had very powerful awakenings, but these experiences, in and of themselves, do not mean that much unless we allow ourselves to be transformed, completely, by what we have discovered. If we try to use them to validate our religious and peer identities and opinions, with our various secret and subtle motives and perceptions so shaped, we corrupt our awakening, and are already entangled in delusion. (And when we make ourselves, or our group or our path or the teacher we've identified ourselves with special, we make ourselves separate.) The most any spiritual institution can do is to support and celebrate what is already real and true without reservation. Profound wisdom and compassion exist anywhere there is total honesty, openness, and willingness.

Full awareness, peace, freedom, clarity and joy can, and do, only exist now. If any of us still find ourselves suffering from the symptoms of ignorance, divisiveness or competition, that is to say, fear, envy, anger, sorrow, frustration, disappointment, jealousy, self-loathing, guilt, depression, loneliness, despair, or confusion, it is because we are still negotiating with Consciousness, still negotiating with God, still negotiating with Truth, still negotiating with Love, still negotiating with Freedom, still negotiating with

Serenity. The pain is none other than the agony of lying to ourselves about what we want more than anything else. It is like finally finding the lover we have always longed for, but holding back in terror of losing that love.

Why put this moment off? That which you seek is That which you already are, and always have been--you are not separate, you cannot be separate from the Absolute, from Infinite Consciousness Itself. If you dare to stop pretending that you and your life are based on some mental version of things that arises out of memory, you will find out beyond any doubt! This is not some kind of wishful thinking or grandiose mental trick. Rather, with total and unflinching sincerity, with no psychological defense or self deception whatsoever, search your heart and find out what you permanently are, what you've been all along. Find out if there has ever been a separate "Other." If you discover there never has been an other, is there one now? Could there ever be? Why pretend anymore?

If you dare to give your heart, your soul, your mind, your body, and your life, unconditionally, to

what you discover to be true, you will know an
infinitely deep and abiding peace that has never
been even a breath away. This bliss, this tranquility
depends on nothing, and It is not capable of ending.
It contains everything and is the source of
everything.

Furthermore, it doesn't make a bit of
difference what you've ever done...or not done. You
can put an end to the battle, Yes, that's correct, just
walk right out of the war, right now. All you have to
do is surrender, not to some authority figure, or
some organization or institution, but surrender,
absolutely and completely and only to your own
deepest Purity.

God and your own Unbounded Love are not
different. If you truly give yourself up completely, it
will shock your whole system. It will suddenly dawn
on you,

"Oh, my God, what a fool I've been!

What have I been thinking?"

Then the absolute insanity of giving yourself to
anything else will become apparent. Why wait?
Why put off your own complete and total liberation?

In your innermost and outermost places, in every
single moment, Love waits for you everywhere. Is
there really anything else you would rather do? Is it
possible that the one thing that you fear the most,
the thing that you avoid the most, is what you truly
desire the most? It cannot abandon you. Even if you
choose to ignore It, trivialize it, betray It and walk
away, It is always closer than your next breath.
Suspend all opinion and debate, and find out for
yourself.

The Bliss of Pure Attention

Question: *Thank you for your kind words and encouragement. One last little question: What feeling is that which affects you so much when you listen to a beautiful piece of music? What sensation is that that consumes your whole being?*

Sometimes a sight or a sound or some particular sensation is so extraordinarily lovely to us that we give it, without deliberation, our undivided attention. But the particular object of attention is only the vehicle. When Consciousness, which is What you are, is not distorted, manipulated, limited, or distracted by some special motive--the attempt to get something, become something, or defend something--the experience of It may be one of exquisite beauty and bliss. It doesn't even make any difference whether you previously judged the object of consciousness as something you liked or something you didn't like. Whether it is called Consciousness or Emptiness or Pure Being or whatever, when there is no longer an infatuation with a separate "you," with its needs, wants, desires, hopes, fears, histories, futures and so on, there is nothing but the intense joy and elegant silence of *what is.*

There Is Only Love

It really doesn't matter
what you've ever done.
Or not done.
It doesn't make any difference
how many times you've deceived yourself
or others.

It doesn't make any difference how many
cheap verbal, intellectual,
and mental imitations
you've sold out for.
It doesn't make any difference
how many times
you've used it, lied about it, betrayed it,
pretended it, or pretended it didn't exist.
It doesn't make any difference how many times
you thought you had lost it.

The only thing that makes any difference at all
is whether you have the honesty

the courage and the humility,

whether you're willing

to be vulnerable enough,

this very moment, to find out what love is.

And when you discover

the vast and endless bliss of it,

whether you are willing to be destroyed by it.

Whether you are willing to disappear into it

now, and to disappear into it forever.

Be honest with yourself:

Is there really something else

you'd rather do?

As much as we'd like to think so,

we can't really "have love."

Simply because it is much bigger

than whatever

we imagine ourselves and our lives to be.

All we can do is immerse ourselves in it.

Drown in it.

Abandon ourselves to it.

For in the end, we don't really exist.
There is only love.
Why not let this be the end?

Let it transform everything.
If your surrender is pure, and complete,
it will change everything immediately.

No longer will the aches of the body nor the
fears and sorrows of the mind trouble you.
For when the body and the mind
are in service to the heart,
it will liberate all of your demons.

I can't tell you exactly how it will be.
You'll have to find out for yourself.
What I do know is that you will see things,
and hear things and feel things
that will bring you to your knees,
passionately weeping
in gratitude and redemption.

We've all been hypocrites and liars.
We've all stolen and used
and hurt and betrayed.
We've all pretended to be
superior and inferior.
Why not let it all end here?

Then things that seemed so important
will have collapsed into thin air.
Did they ever really exist in the first place?

And you will find yourself seeing
and loving people, places and things
you didn't even know existed.

And you'll wonder
"How could I have fooled myself so?"
And you will see everything
new and fresh and clear.
And a calm and a deep joy
will pervade the entire universe.

Love Is Everywhere

Everywhere you turn,

there is the lover you have always wanted.

The mother you always wanted.

The father you always wanted.

The child you always wanted.

The brother or sister you always wanted.

The universe is full of intimate friends,

and you may have been missing it.

They have always been there--

you just may not have noticed,

because you were looking for them

in some other form.

(Maybe they were in disguise.)

If you want to find out if that is so, stop pretending

you already know anybody,

or anything about them,

and look slowly, deeply, with great curiosity,

into the eyes of the next person you meet:
your lover, your spouse, a colleague at work,
the checkout clerk at the convenience store,
or somebody on the street,
even your own eyes.
Regardless of what they say or do,
speak only to that love,
that father or mother, that child.
Speak only to that person.
Speak only to that one.

Perhaps you've already noticed it:
that no matter who it is,
there's always somebody in there.
When you go past the surface, mechanical,
habitual level on which we normally operate
and, with great care,
go to the trouble of finding out who is in there,
the results are always
thrilling, shocking, astonishing.
All you have to do is look.
Who would have imagined that to be so?
Everybody is waiting to be found.

It is a very delicate matter, however, and it
requires a very subtle awareness and sensitivity.
It demands great intelligence, and there cannot
be any hidden vested interests or hopes for
some kind of self-gratification.

If there are, you will probably miss it.
So don't take it casually, or half-heartedly.
No matter what form or appearance it takes,
however, it is always amazing.

The Friend of all strangers,
the Lover of all lovers
is always right here.
Right here, waiting to be seen.
Find out for yourself. (Don't miss it!)
It is everywhere and in everybody.

For information on future publications, books, tapes,
counseling programs, intensives, and retreats with
Scott Morrison, as well as hundreds of online
commentaries, talks, and dialogues

visit us at

Awakening On This Breath

www.openmindopenheart.org/

or write us at

staff@openmindopenheart.org
